# WHEELS of COMMERCE:
## MONEY CIRCULATES

**VIRGINIA HAMMON**
Author, designer, piecemaker

Quilted by Coleen Barnhardt
Inspiration pattern by Willyne Hammerstein
Bound by Cris Pera with Leon and Lewis

## ACKNOWLEDGMENTS

This quilt was a lot of fun to make – shopping for the fabrics, selecting the pieces, discovering the designs that formed, and then sewing together more than 8,000 little seams by hand. While I concentrated on this, family and friends kept me afloat. Special thanks to sister Rosalind Hamar who kept me fed; sons, Darius Monsef who kept the lights on and Cyrus Monsef who kept my car running; cousin Jan Sturtevant who has a good eye for design and who helped make the great quilting possible; meticulous craftsperson and artistic consultant Cris Pera who bound the quilt, with help from cats, Lewis and Leon; and quilter extraordinaire Coleen Barnhardt who took my piecemaking to the next level. Geri Grasvik at my home base quilt fabric store, The Pine Needle in Lake Oswego, Oregon, has also been a long-time cheerleader of my efforts. Christopher Brooks did the book design and graciously put up with last-minute demands. Photography is by Dan Kvitka Photography. My family, friends and fellow members of the Portland Modern Quilt Guild kept my spirits up and my determination solid over the many years I've been working on this project.

The *Wheels of Commerce* quilt was inspired by and partially follows a pattern by Willyne Hammerstein in her book, *Millefiori Quilts*, published by QuiltMania (2011). I've added almost 10 'wheels' and put it together slightly differently.

Copyright 2017 by Virginia Hammon. All rights reserved.
Library of Congress cataloging – in Publication Data
Hammon, Virginia 1948-
    *Wheels of Commerce: Money Circulates* / Virginia Hammon
    p. cm.
ISBN: 978-0-97-860072-3
Art Quilts. 2. Quilting. 3. Monetary Policy
Published by Great Democracy Media, Portland, Oregon

Set in Questa Sans

WHEELS OF COMMERCE, 2017 (81" x 83") BY VIRGINIA HAMMON

## MONEY CIRCULATES AND PROPELS THE WHEELS OF COMMERCE

*Wheels of Commerce* is a quilt that stars in a greater effort – another book that explains the money system that we have chosen and its consequences, and that makes a case for choosing an alternative. That book, *US Money: Piecing Together a Better Alternative*, is illustrated with 50 quilts – publishing date is January 2018. This book is offered with hope that it piques your curiosity and you will watch for and buy the *US Money* book when it is published.

I slowed the completion of the illustrative quilts for the *US Money* book when I decided to make this English paper pieced quilt, *Wheels of Commerce*. It is put together entirely by hand and took about 1500 hours. As I worked, I reflected on all I had learned about money. I realized that the most important thing about money – which we sometimes forget or misunderstand – is that it circulates. Wealth can belong to you, to me or to us, and each of us can keep track of our income and wealth with two-dimensional accounts – an income statement (revenue, expense, net income), and a balance sheet (assets, debts, net worth). Money can be a form of wealth and we can keep track of its ownership in those accounts. In the two dimensions of accounting, one plus one must alway equals two. But, for the economy as a whole, money also serves as a reusable tool, constantly circulating in our economy, facilitating exchanges. In money's role as a circulating tool, it doesn't fit neatly into a two-dimensional accounting model. In circulation, one plus one plus one may equal five.

Here I offer three short stories to illustrate what it means to be three-dimensional money. The first story, *The Stranger*, has been around since the Great Depression. I wrote the second two.

To accompany the pictures of the wheels of the quilt, I've added some miscellaneous information about money and commerce. Thanks for buying this book and reading it.

## THE STRANGER

In a small town in the middle of America times were tough. Nearly everyone was out of work and in debt. People had very little money, and not enough to prosper.

One day a stranger came into town and stopped at the lone hotel. He set a $100 bill on the counter and told the innkeeper he'd like to look at the rooms before deciding whether he wanted to stay. But, first, if the innkeeper didn't mind, his journey had been long and he'd like a quick nap in the Inn's lounge before checking out the rooms. The Inn was empty and the rooms were unlocked, so the innkeeper said, *"Please, feel free. The lounge is ahead, the rooms are upstairs, and the stairs are at the back of the building. I have some business I must attend, and will be back shortly."*

The man went into the lounge and settled in for a nap. The innkeeper grabbed the $100 bill and ran with it to the restaurant next door to pay his tab. The restaurant owner ran with the $100 to the butcher and paid his overdue balance. The butcher took it and ran to the grocer to pay his bill. The grocer took it and ran to the town produce farmer to restock his shelves. The farmer took it and ran to the quilt shop to buy fabric for a quilt. The quilt store owner took it and ran to buy frame materials from the hardware store. The hardware store owner took the $100 to pay the prostitute he'd been seeing on credit. She took the bill and ran to pay off the innkeeper for her use of his rooms. She had just slapped the $100 bill back down on the counter paying off her debt, when the stranger arrived back at the desk.

He said he had decided he would not stay. Pulling some matches and a cigar out of his pocket, he lit the $100 bill and then his cigar, saying with a wink, *"It's just a gag gift from a friend."*

When the stranger left, the town settled back into its stagnant economy.[1]

## THE BANKER

In a small town in the middle of America times were tough. Nearly everyone was out of work and in debt. People had very little money, and not enough to prosper.

One day a fancy car pulling a glitzy trailer came into town. The car parked on Main Street. A man got out and walked up and down Main Street. He found an empty store front he liked and signed a lease. He spruced up the building with fresh paint, furnishings from his trailer, and an impressive big safe. A sign was painted on the window, *"Banker's Bank – We make loans so the community can prosper."* He held an open house to introduce himself and his loan program. Nearly everyone came.

The Banker explained that they could open accounts in his bank. He would keep their money safe for them and guarantee that all their money would be available whenever they needed it. The banker would provide valuable services – store their money safely, transfer it to others on their instructions, and keep an account for them.

Then the banker introduced his most important service – a service that could increase economic activity and bring prosperity to all. He would lend them money for a small interest fee. The money that they borrowed would be special money; it would be *banker money*. This banker money was his promise that it would be as good as ordinary money; it could be used interchangeably and he would guarantee they could always access the money they kept in their account. As long as they all agreed to honor his banker money for exchanges, it would make them all prosperous. The townspeople decided to use his banker money in addition to their own.

The townspeople brought in the little money that they had, opened accounts and deposited their own money. They took away check books or debit cards that let them use their money to buy from others in the community. And, most of the people took out loans, thinking with a little extra money, they could make more and pay the banker back the loan. They deposited their borrowed money in the bank too. All the loans were due in a year and a day.

The town prospered. There was more money for buying and selling. All the money circulated again and again. There was enough money so all the services or goods people could offer found buyers. Everyone was working and earning to capacity and living comfortably.

At the end of the year, the banker called in all the loans and the interest due. The amount of banker money in circulation matched the amount of the banker loans and the townspeople were able to pay back all of the banker money they had borrowed. But no banker money had been created to pay the interest. The interest had to be paid with the little ordinary money that the townspeople had before the banker arrived. After returning the banker money and paying the interest on their loans, the town had no more money at all. The banker packed up his belongings, his banker money, and the interest money. Then he left town.

When the banker left with all their money, the town settled back into its stagnant economy.

## WE THE PEOPLE

In a small town in the middle of America times were tough. Nearly everyone was out of work and in debt. People had no money, and prosperity was just a broken dream.

But, they'd had two lessons in the nature of money: one from a stranger and one from a banker. They called a community meeting to discuss what they had learned. They now knew that the most important characteristic of money was the agreement of the community to use it for their transactions. And they knew that when there was the right amount of money moving around in the economy, they could all prosper. They decided if stranger money could bring a burst of prosperity, and if banker money could bring prosperity for a year, then, if they created their own money they could prosper indefinitely.

So they created town money and called it *US money*, because it brought prosperity *"for all of us."*

The townspeople decided that it would take a base of 15,000 money units per person to have a prosperous economy and a healthy life for all. They created enough to distribute that amount to everyone in the community on the first day of the year. And they did. When people received their share, they spent it over the year. Some people got by on their allotment; that's all they spent. But once they spent it, it circulated. Some people invested, produced, sold many goods and services, and acquired great wealth. Some paid for education and training and increased their earning potential. Everyone had enough to meet their basic needs. No one in the community went hungry and everyone had a roof over their head. Anxiety, stress, ill health and violence all went down. The community was healthier than it had ever been before.

The money circulated, just as the stranger's money and the banker's money had circulated. The 15,000 units that went to one person was used in dozens of exchanges over the year. The total economic activity was many times more than the money they had created. Every individual who had more money come in than their basic allotment of 15,000 units paid a simple 10% tax on that additional income at the end of the year. This was easy to do as the number of transactions was on average far more than the 15,000 units per person. This 10% tax was enough so that the town could turn around and reissue the basic income to all their citizens the next year. And, the cycle repeated.

The wheels of commerce were set in perpetual motion.

**NO. 1**

**MONEY AND HAPPINESS**

## TIGER

1914 – a year of the Tiger – is the first year the current money system was put into practice by the Federal Reserve Act, passed in December 1913. Tigers are considered to be brave, cruel, forceful, stately and terrifying. They are the *symbol* of power and lordliness – not a bad description of the American dollar.

Andrew Jackson (1767–1845), the 7TH president of the United States is on the $20 bill. He has a mixed record: successful general, defender of the common man, and defender of commonwealth money (as opposed to banker money primarily issued by Northern interests), slave owner, forceful and deadly remover of native Americans from their lands. He will be replaced sometime in the next decade or so by Harriet Tubman, slave, civil rights activist, civil war spy and military leader who freed 700 slaves.

## CROWN

Money is a token that is recognizable, authentic and securable. It must be trustworthy. It requires community-wide agreement that it will be used as money. Through history, this agreement has been made by some form of community governance. And up until the most recent centuries, agreement was often imposed by a crowned head of state.

## THE US DOLLAR

The Annual Financial Reports of the Federal Reserve show that the supply of American dollars has grown at an average annual rate of 7.8% since 1913.[2]

## YOU MAKE ME HAPPY

Does money make us happy? A 2010 Princeton study found that up to $75,000, people said they were happier with more (in today's dollars, adjusted for cost of living in each state ranges from $65,000 to $120,000). The lower their income fell below that benchmark, the unhappier they reported being.[3]

**NO. 2**
## THE WIZARD OF OZ

## BUTTERFLIES

In chaos theory, the butterfly effect means a small change can result in large differences in a later state. Our 1913 choice of money system is a determining foundation of the state of the Union today.

## THE POWERFUL OZ

Oz is the abbreviation for ounce. In 1964, educator and historian Henry Littlefield described *The Wonderful Wizard of Oz* by L. Frank Baum (1900) as a parable about money reform and the 1890s Midwestern political movement led by William Jennings Bryan (1860–1925), three times candidate for President of the United States. Others have added a political interpretation of this delightful story. Dorothy, representing everyman, is eventually saved from the power of the bankers behind the curtain by her silver slippers, which represent a money created by and for the people themselves.[4]

## KNIVES, FORKS AND SPOONS

Food is the base of the economy – survival. In the past two and a half decades, U.S. households in the lowest income quintile (the poorest 20 percent of households) spent between 29 and 43 percent of their annual before-tax income on food, compared to 7–9 percent spent by households in the highest income quintile. (Before tax income includes earnings and other money income, public assistance, Supplemental Security Income payments, and Supplemental Nutrition Assistance Program (SNAP) benefits.[5]

NO. 3
OWN IT ALL!

## ZERO

Zero represents the state of total absence or neutrality. Nearly every spiritual practice in the world encourages some form of letting go of the material world, emptying the mind to seek enlightenment. Overwhelming attachment to wealth is viewed as a handicap.

## OWN IT ALL

According to the nonprofit Oxfam International, in January 2017, eight men own the same wealth as the 3.6 billion people who make up the poorest half of humanity. While the wealth of the poorest half of the world's population has fallen by a trillion dollars since 2010, a drop of 38 percent, the wealth of the richest 62 people on the planet has increased by more than half a trillion dollars to $1.76 trillion.[6]

## TELEPHONES

In just 10 years, smart phones have replaced dozens of other pieces of technology, from cameras, computers, GPS, portable music players, calculators, radio, video and voice recorders, eBook readers, flashlight, compass, credit card scanner, portable video players. The astounding speed from invention to ubiquitous gives us hope for taking rapid action to preserve humanity and the planet when we decide to give it our all.

## THINGS

Research over the last decade finds: if you want to be happier, invest in experiences or products that help you create experiences. Buying things is often followed by buyer's remorse, or losing interest. And one is more tempted to unfavorably and unhappily compare what one has with what others have – which can't be done with an experience.[7]

**NO. 4**

**THE RICHEST OF THE RICH**

## BIRDS

In 2016, the Audubon society reported that thirty percent of North American Bird species have declined since 1966. The Tri-national North American Bird Conservation Initiative (NABCI) reported that more than one-third of North American bird species are at risk of extinction unless significant conservation actions are taken.[8]

## AIRPLANES

Commercial aviation in the US in 2017 brought in $743 billion in revenues, expensed $687 billion, for an operating profit of $56 billion. Net profits were $31 billion, providing a return on investment of 8.8 percent. Passenger travel accounted for $527 billion and cargo $51 billion. They could afford to make those seats a little roomier and more comfortable.[9]

## STAR POWER – THE TOP 1%

While the United States has the most wealth in the world, it also has the highest wealth inequality. In 2015, just 20 people owned as much wealth as the poorest half of all Americans (152 million people living in 47 million households). The 2016 Allianze Global Wealth Report looks at the share of national wealth assets held by the middle class. Slovakia comes in first with over 60%. The US comes in last at 22%.[10]

A 2009 study published in the British Medical Journal found that unequally skewed income levels in the 15 wealthy countries they studied corresponded with 893,914 avoidable deaths per year. Severe inequality kills.[11][12]

## NO. 5
## SPACE INVADERS

## SPACE INVADERS

In 2015, the world spent $91.5 billion on video games. Americans spent $23.5 billion.[13] A 2014 Oxford University study found that children who play video games for one hour or less per day tend to be more social and satisfied with life than kids who don't play at all. Between one and three hours there is no discernible effect, positive or negative. Over three hours and children are less social and less satisfied with life, and more likely to have negative behavior issues.[14]

## USB

In 2016, 87% of Americans went online to connect with friends and family, shop, get news and search for information. The offline population has declined rapidly from 48% in 2000 to 13% in 2016. Age and income are most likely to determine who isn't online.[15]

## GEORGE WASHINGTON

George Washington was the first US president. He was first put on the one-dollar bill in 1869, seven years after the bill was put into print. The average dollar bill's lifespan is just 18 months due to heavy wear and tear.

**NO. 6**

**WEB OF CARGO**

## THE WEB OF SEA COMMERCE

Ninety-five percent of world cargo volume moves by ship. In 1999, WIRED magazine wrote a fascinating article about the transformation of sea cargo shipping. Shipping containers and the way that the worldwide web works changed the way shippers think. WIRED wrote, *"At its heart, ocean shipping is a network business, just like airlines and telecommunications. Passengers, bulk goods, data — all three represent uniform-size cargo, shooting through global transport and sorting systems 24/7/365. Viewed this way, airline seats, data packets, and 40-foot shipping containers are much the same — commoditized units for carrying content."*

On the communications web, digital packets of information take the most open and fastest route from one point to another. This might mean that your email goes from your computer to London and New Delhi before it reaches your friend in the next state. It's moving at the speed of light and the longer journey makes no appreciable difference to you or the recipient. Some clever shippers realized that they could treat shipping containers the same way. Using computers to track all container ships and their itineraries, they could ship on the fastest most available combination of ships and routes. Like an email, a shipment from San Francisco to China might go through Peru. This change in shipping method means things ship faster and more cheaply.

Cheaper shipping means we can afford produce and products shipped from far away. I ordered one ball of yarn from Florida and a package of 8 balls of similar yarn from Turkey. The cost was about the same, and the yarn from Turkey arrived first. This changes commerce.[16]

NO. 7
ALIEN BABIES

## ALIEN BABIES

(With tongue in cheek, this fabric represents immigration. The fabric was designed and is sold on Spoonflower by quilt collector and historian, Bill Volckening.) Our current money system requires an increasing population. It grows the supply of money at an average annual rate just under 8%. To accommodate this increase in the money supply, economic productivity and population must also increase. By the 1960s the fertility rate in the US had leveled off, as is common in wealthy economies. We were making enough babies to barely keep our population numbers at a steady level. To increase population enough to help absorb the growing money supply and curb inflation, the US increased immigration (both legally, and by turning a blind eye to illegal immigration). Immigrants, who are often poor, have higher fertility rates. In our current money system, this higher fertility rate is good because it adds further to the required population growth.

Unless we change our money system, leveling off or reducing our population will harm the economy. I explain more about why in my book, *US Money*.[17][18]

## SKULLS

(These glow in the dark!) Poverty kills. A June 2011 article in The American Journal of Public Health reported a study calculating the number of deaths attributable to six social factors, including low income. For 2000, the study attributed 176,000 deaths to racial segregation and 133,000 to individual poverty. For comparison, 119,000 people in the United States die from accidents each year, and 156,000 from lung cancer. Poverty is as much a public health issue as accidents and smoking. All unnecessary and early deaths impact communities, not just individuals.[19]

## NO. 8
## ALL HANDS ON DECK

## BUGS

At any time, an estimated 10 quintillion (10,000,000,000,000,000,000) individual insects are alive. In the US, there are approximately 91,000 described species. On Earth there are more than 1.5 million — three times the number of all other animals combined. Insects play an important role in the food web — as a food source for other animals, and as pollinators of many of our fruits, flowers, and vegetables. Insects break down and dispose of wastes, dead animals and plants. Our world would be very unpleasant without their service.[20][21]

## HANDS ON DECK

World population is about 7.5 billion. If everyone in the world consumed at the rate that we do in the US, it would take 2.5 Earths to provide the resources. In 2017, the US consumed all that our Earth can renew in a year by June 10th. For the remaining half of the year, we liquidate our stocks of resources — overfish, harvest forests, import more than we export, and accumulate more carbon dioxide in the atmosphere than our ecosystems can absorb.[22]

## GOLDEN SHOWERS & THE MAD TEA PARTY

In 1896, Presidential candidate William Jennings Bryan described two ideas of government: The Republican idea that when legislation makes the rich richer, their prosperity will *"leak through on those down below"*; and, the Democratic idea that when legislation makes the masses prosperous their prosperity *"will find its way up and through every class that rests upon it."* [23]

In 1932, humorist Will Rogers jokingly referred to the Republican economic philosophy as *trickle down*. The name stuck. President Reagan's advisers thought trickle down was a hard sell, so they renamed their tax cuts for the rich *supply-side economics,* or *Reaganomics*. Under Reagan, taxes for the wealthiest Americans dropped from 70 percent down to 28 percent. (... up briefly to 39.6 percent under H.W. Bush, down to 35 percent under G.W. Bush, up to 39.6 percent under Obama.) This distinction is still apt. A recent Republican movement to reduce taxes on the rich, shrink government, and eliminate protective regulations took the name, *Tea Party*. [24]

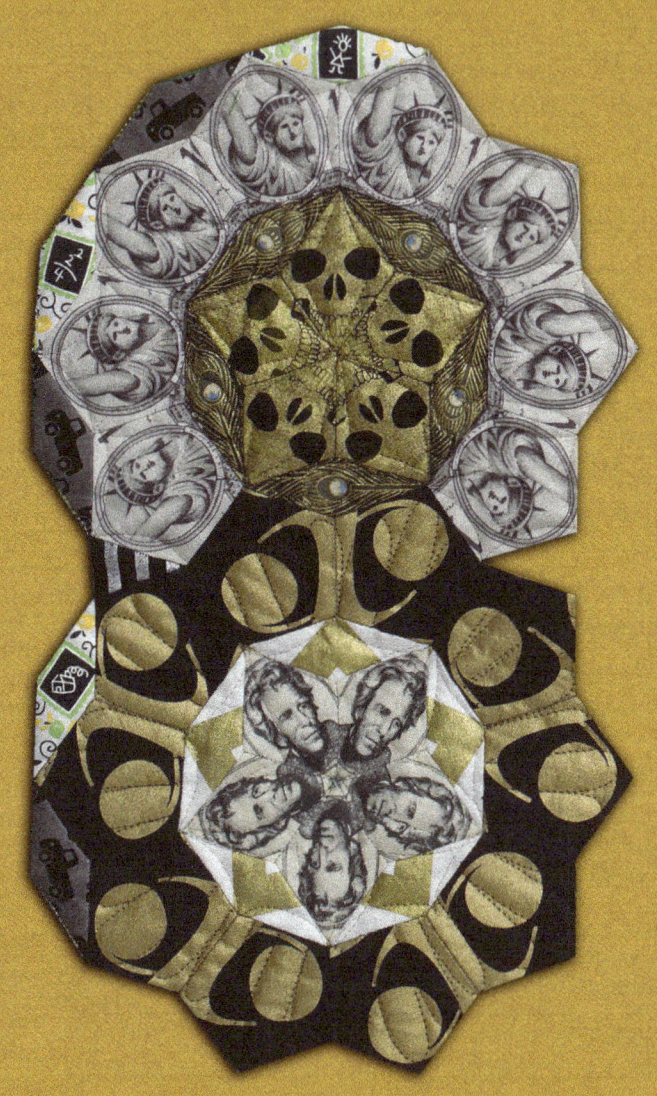

NO. 9

**FERTILITY AND ABUNDANCE**

## FERTILITY

Ninety-five percent of our food comes from the soil. Our lives depend on the fertility of our soil, adequate water, and good weather. Scientific American reports that generating three centimeters of top soil takes 1,000 years, and if current rates of degradation continue all of the world's top soil could be gone within 60 years. We've already destroyed one third of the Earth's topsoil and the destruction is accelerating. The causes of soil destruction include chemical-heavy farming techniques, deforestation which increases erosion, and global warming.[25]

Agriculture, food, and related industries contributed $992 billion to U.S. gross domestic product (GDP) in 2015, a 5.5-percent share. The output of America's farms contributed $136.7 billion of this sum — about 1 percent of GDP. The cost of the loss of topsoil and other environmental degradation is not factored into the costs of our food; that's left to the future.

In good news the demand for organic food has been growing by double digits every year.[26]

## TRUCKING IN OUR FOOD

While bringing food from far away doesn't add much to the cost we pay at the supermarket, there is a heavy price to pay in carbon-footprint and its resulting environmental degradation. And there are many advantages to eating food grown locally: Local foods are fresher and seasonal; they are more delicious and nutrient-dense; they need no storage or artificial ripening; and, there is less chance of contamination when foods take a shorter route from farm to table. Short-term, eating organic, local food may cost a little more, but long-term, it saves healthcare costs and lives.

More good news: the number of farmers' markets has grown steadily, from about 1,755 in 1994 when the USDA began to track them, to over 8,144 in 2013.

## NO. 10
## GOLD AND THE KEY TO FINANCIAL SUCCESS

## GOLD MONEY

Gold money is a commodity money; it has a value in the marketplace as a commodity and it has a value as money.

## A KEY TO FINANCIAL SUCCESS

Gold money, or gold as a standard for the value of money has been promoted by those of great wealth. The very wealthy can control gold's value in the marketplace by hoarding it and running up the price, or dumping a lot into the marketplace which makes its value go down. By controlling the value of gold as money, the very rich control the value of everything in the marketplace – an unequaled advantage. They like a gold money system because it makes it easier for them to increase their wealth and political power. However in the last 800 years or so, they found an even better way to shift wealth from ordinary people into the pockets of a very few – our current money system.[27]

NO. 11
AT WORK

## AT WORK

The role of labor in the economy is changing as more jobs are automated, computerized or globalized. According to an October 2014 Jobs report, more than 92 million Americans – 37 percent of the civilian population aged 16 and over – are neither employed nor unemployed, but fall in the category of *not in the labor force*. Of these adults, 93 percent did not want a job. This included a rising number of 16- to 24-year-olds, up to an average of 40 percent. It included a smaller increase among prime working-age adults (ages 25 to 54) to 17 percent. And, as one might expect people 55 and over make up more than half of the 85.9 million adults who say they do not want a job.

In June 2017, the average unemployment rate – people who want a job and can't find one – in the US was 4.4 percent. It varied state by state from a low of 2.3 in Colorado to 6.8 percent in Alaska.[28]

## SLOTH TIME

Americans get the least vacation time of any wealthy nation. Other countries enjoy as many as 40 days off a year with pay; the US is the only country where employers are not required to give their employees *any* paid time off. Some Americans get 10 days of national holidays off, but some don't get any time off – paid or otherwise.

Europeans do quite well. UK workers enjoy 28 days, Poland-26, while Austria, Denmark, Finland, France, Greece, Luxembourg and Sweden all get 25 paid days off as standard. These are all healthy economies. They find that adequate time off means employees come back to work refreshed, de-stressed, healthier and more productive.[29]

A salary.com survey found 89 percent of the workforce wastes some time at work, and roughly 4 percent of the workforce spends about half their time at work doing non-work related activities.[30]

**NO. 12**

**SEEDS TO SHIRTS**

## SEEDS

In 1903, commercial seed houses offered hundreds of varieties, including 497 varieties of lettuce, 408 of tomatoes, and 307 kinds of corn. By 1983 93 percent of the varieties had gone extinct. Many varieties mean more adaptability to varying conditions.[31]

## HOUSING

The US has roughly 117 million households (people living together-families) with an average of 2.64 people per household. There are 136 million housing units for a population of 323 million. Sixty-four percent are owner occupied (2011–2015). The median value of owner-occupied housing units from 2011–2015 was $178,600.[32]

## COTTON CLOTH

Cotton is a fiber that grows around a cottonseed. Fragments of cotton fabric have been found in the Indus Valley that are between 7,000 and 8,000 years old. Today cotton crops take up about 2.5 percent of the world's arable land, but use 16–25 percent of the world's insecticides and 11 percent of the pesticides. For every nine ounces of cotton – about 2 yards of light quilting fabric – growers use an average of 17 teaspoons of chemical fertilizers and nearly a teaspoon of active ingredients, including pesticides, herbicides, insecticides and defoliants. Many of these chemicals are known carcinogens. They kill bees, harm wildlife and get into our water and food and harm us. The supply of organically farmed cotton is growing by the double digits as awareness and demand increase.[33] [34]

NO. 13

**ONE IN MANY**

## FINGERPRINTS & ID

1858   Sir William Herschel, British Administrator in India required fingerprints and signatures on civil contracts.
1891   Juan Vucetich, an Argentine Police Official, was the first to use fingerprinting to identify a criminal.
1908   The US Military adopts the use of fingerprints.
1911   Fingerprints were first accepted by US courts as a reliable means of identification.
1924   The FBI began collecting, preserving, classifying and exchanging fingerprint records.
1980   The first computer data base of fingerprints was developed, now knows as the Integrated Automated Fingerprint Identification System (IAFIS).

Today, the IAFIS has about 70 million sets of prints. Dead people are removed when their data is submitted by a coroner. A few decades back anyone over the age of 65 who hadn't been arrested or imprisoned in 10 years was assumed to be dead or not an active criminal and removed from the file. Now the age limit has been increased.[35][36]

## SALMON PORTLAND CHASE (1808–1873)

Salmon Portland Chase played a significant role in introducing paper money in the US. He was the Secretary of the Treasury in 1862 when a national banking network was established and true sovereign money – the Greenback – was introduced and used for the duration of the Civil War. Chase had political ambitions and so put his own portrait on the on the $1 Greenback.

Chase was honored for his contribution to the money system with his portrait on the $10,000 bill, first printed in 1924 – the highest denomination ever offered to the public. These bills were last printed in 1969 and by 2009, there were only 336 known in existence, most with collectors or in museums. Chase Manhattan Bank was named for him, though he had no financial connection to the bank.[37]

**NO. 14**

**THE VALUABLE DOLLAR**

## DOLLAR

Our current money is an IOU from the private banking system, authorized as *legal tender* by our government. Our paper money reads, *Federal Reserve Note*. A *note* is an IOU. Our money is an IOU from our private banking sector. How this happens is explained in *US Money*: *Piecing Together a Better Alternative* (2018).

## POLLINATORS

In 2014, beekeepers reported a 34.2 percent decline from the prior year. In 2015, the reported decline in the number of bees was 44 percent. This dramatic decline is continuing. A growing body of evidence points to one class of pesticides in particular, *neonicotinoids*, as the culprit to the massive bee die-offs. The European Union banned the three most widely used neonicotinoids in 2013, but they are still used widely in the US. Since the ban in Europe, the European Union has seen a significant increase in healthy bee colonies.[38]

## WHAT DOES $1 BUY?

We keep track of the changing value of the dollar. The Consumer Price Indexes (CPI) program, maintained at the US Bureau of Labor Statistics *"produces monthly data on changes in the prices paid by urban consumers for a representative basket of goods."* This index is important because the government uses changes in the index to calculate payment increases in some government spending (e.g. Social Security payments, private contractor payments). How these indexes are calculated has changed over the years. Shadowstats.com presents a cogent argument that the CPI *"has been reconfigured since early 1980s to understate inflation versus common experience"* – to keep reported inflation lower than it is.[39] [40]

**NO. 15**

# GROCERY CARTS

## FRUITS AND VEGETABLES

Eating green and red vegetables is important for good health and long life. In 2017, the scientists at the Imperial College of London analyzed 95 studies on fruit and vegetable intake. Their meta-analysis included 2 million people from populations worldwide. The analysis found that eating any amount of fruit and vegetables daily improves health outcomes. Eating 10 portions of fruits and vegetables per day was tied to a:

- 33% reduced risk of stroke;
- 31% reduced risk of premature death;
- 28% reduced risk of cardiovascular disease;
- 24% reduced risk of heart disease;
- 13% reduced risk of cancer.[41]

## GROCERY CARTS

Grocery shopping is changing. Farmer's markets, Community Supported Agriculture (CSAs-farm shares, delivery to home), meal kit delivery services, and online shopping are transforming the way we get our food. Amazon, which boasts a 5 percent share of total retail sales (excluding food) and 35 percent share of online sales, bought Whole Foods in July 2017. This will have an impact on local grocery stores.

## FOOD CARGO

The British Guardian magazine did some interesting research in 2003. They bought a basket of 20 fresh foods from a grocery store and calculated how many miles they had come. The total miles traveled by all their items was 100,943 miles. The food came from a few miles for local beef to 14,287 miles for Wine from New Zealand. A 2001 study by Iowa State University's Leopold Center for Sustainable Agriculture found that Chicago's food comes an average of 1,500 miles.[42] [43]

## NO. 16
## STORM TROOPERS

## CROCODILES AND STORM TROOPERS

In the US, thirty-three percent of the federal government operating fund (funded by individual and corporate taxes) is spent by the Departments of Defense ($635 billion – 2016) and Homeland Security ($60 billion – 2016). More is spent by the Departments of Energy and NASA, but it is nearly impossible to figure out how much. Another $39 billion is spent by the Defense Security Cooperation Agency to train and coordinate with other militaries around the world and to market weapons and munitions to potential buyers. In comparison, in 2016, we spent:

| | |
|---|---|
| $33 BILLION | on Housing and Urban Development, |
| $32 BILLION | on our Department of Justice, |
| $30 BILLION | on our Department of State, |
| $19 BILLION | on the Department of the Interior, |
| $13 BILLION | on the US Agency for International Development, |
| $12 BILLION | on the Department of Commerce, |
| $9 BILLION | on the Environmental Protection Agency[44] |

The US spends more on military than anyone else in the world, and roughly 34 percent of the total spent by all nations. The US spends more than the next seven nations combined. Our expenditures are nearly three times higher than China ($216 billion), the second-highest nation, and more than seven times third place Russia ($85 billion.)[45]

## BIRDS AND BEES – THE ECONOMY OF POLLINATORS

Around 30 percent of the food Americans consume is produced from bee pollinated plant life. It's closer to 35% globally. Pollinators contribute more than $24 billion to the US economy. In just the past few years beekeepers in the US have collectively lost an estimated 10 million beehives at an approximate current value of $200 each. The cost of renting honey bee hives for almond pollination rose from about $50 in 2003 to $200 by 2014.[46][47]

**NO. 17**

**HOLDING IT ALL TOGETHER**

## HOLDING IT TOGETHER

A growing body of science, including the work of Harvard University's Center for the Developing Child, has found that toxic stress can impede healthy development, literally changing children's brains and affecting their capacity to absorb even the best instruction. Common stressors are food insecurity, substandard housing, greater exposure to violence, and family health problems. Adults respond to stress in the same way; stress reduces cognitive function, causes disease and leads to an earlier death.[48]

## MEDITATION AT SCHOOL AND WORK

Mindfulness, which can be practiced by itself, or as part of meditation or prayer, shrinks the amygdala and thickens the pre-frontal cortex of the brain. This strengthens connectivity between areas of the brain that support attention and concentration, and weakens the amygdala's capacity to hijack the thinking parts of the brain with undo emotional stress reactions (higher blood pressure, measurable changes in kidney, heart and liver function).

This reduction in stress is good for learning and good for doing. Both schools and businesses have been experimenting with meditation and found that it improves performance and health. The Momentous School in Texas has 20 years of data on practicing mindfulness with children that shows impressive improvements in academic and emotional development. Other schools and businesses are incorporating mindfulness practice into their days with equal success.[49] [50] [51] [52] [53]

**NO. 18**
**LINCOLN & SLAVES**

## LINCOLN MEMORIAL

The Lincoln Memorial was built to honor the 16TH President of the US (1861–1865), Abraham Lincoln. The current US $5 bill has President Lincoln's portrait on the front and the Lincoln Memorial on the back. The memorial has come to be symbolic of race relations. In 1963 Martin Luther King, Jr. gave his famous *"I Have a Dream"* speech from its steps.[54]

## MINIONS

A minion is *"a follower or underling of a powerful person, especially a servile or unimportant one."* Our current money system gives the power to rule the nation to a small number of very wealthy people – depriving the rest of us of some very significant choices, and making us minions to those who rule.[55][56]

## MOUSE & CHEESE

Our current money system by its design, shifts wealth to the few individuals who have the power to create new money for the supply. The rest of us are cheese in their trap – explained in *US Money* (2018).

## NO. 19 AND 20
## SWEET LAND OF LIBERTY

## STATUE OF LIBERTY

The president of the French Anti-Slavery Society, Edouard de Laboulaye, came up with the idea for the Statue of Liberty sometime between 1865–1870. He was an ardent supporter of the Union in the American Civil War and wanted to honor the abolition of slavery and what he saw as the emergence of true freedom and democracy for all. He hoped that by calling attention to the US achievements, it would inspire the French people to call for their own democracy.[57]

## DEATHS

From 1526 to 1867, the period of the Atlantic Slave Trade, some 12.5 million slaves were shipped from Africa to the Americas. Only 10.7 million arrived. Many died in route. About 3 percent of the total, some 390,000 people made it to North American soil. By the Civil War about 4 million people lived in slavery. Half of their babies died in slavery – twice the rate for non-slave babies.[58][59]

## ANDREW JACKSON (1767–1845), US PRESIDENT

Unfortunately, our Constitution fails to clearly state who has the power to create our nation's money. So, the money creation power has been a bone of contention, especially in our country's early years. Andrew Jackson considered a chartered, privately-owned bank with the power to create new money for the nation to be the main threat to our Republic. Jackson fought hard for a money created directly by the government, but he lost this battle. The story of banks, bankers, and the US government is a fascinating read. *The Lost Science of Money* by Stephen Zarlenga (2002) is a great read for history buffs.

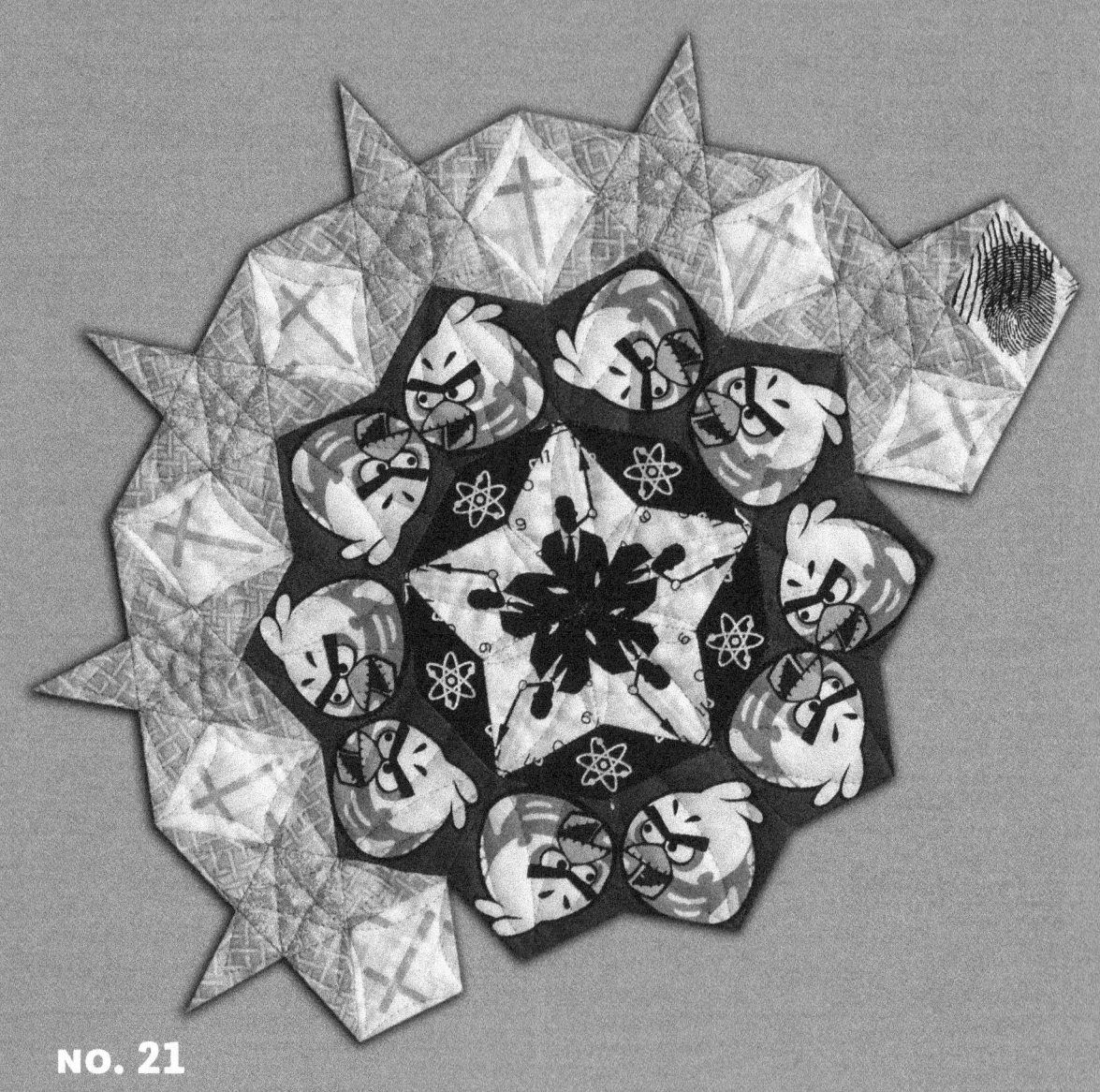

**NO. 21**
# ANGRY BIRDS
------------

## SCIENCE RESEARCH AND DEVELOPMENT (R&D)

In the 1960s, an average of 15 percent of the US federal government operating fund budget went to research and development. Defense R&D was an average of 12 percent of Defense spending. Non-defense R&D was 22 percent of non-defense spending — a whopping investment in fueling innovation! In the 2010s, our average total federal operating fund spending on R&D has averaged 11 percent (11.8 percent of defense spending, and 10.2 percent of non-defense spending). So, we continue to invest about the same in defense research and development, but we have cut our investment in non-defense research and development in half.[60]

## ANGRY BIRDS

Angry Birds is a video game franchise created by Finnish company Rovio Entertainment. The series focuses on multi-colored birds who try to save their eggs from green-colored pigs (metaphor intended?). The game was introduced in 2009 and by July 2015 it had been downloaded more than three billion times, making it the most downloaded *freemium* game series of all time. (Freemium is a new word-concept for pricing a product or service with a free basic function, and charging money for premium features.)[61]

## CHRISTIANITY IN AMERICA

After the 1929 market crash and the decade long Great Depression, Americans had very unfavorable attitudes towards unfettered capitalism, big corporations, and the very rich few who owned them. Corporations tried PR campaigns to change public opinion and it didn't work. They turned to churches. Corporations from General Motors to Hilton Hotels bankrolled clergymen to attack the New Deal as a program of *pagan statism*, *Stalinesque socialism* or *communism*. They gave prizes to clergy for sermons that equated religious freedom with capitalism, deregulation, small government and Libertarianism. They sent these sermons to churches across the nation. Over decades, they succeeded in politicizing many churches, getting them to throw the support of the pulpit behind unfettering big business and allowing it to exploit the nation with minimum regulation. Kevin Kruse's book, *One Nation Under God; How Corporate America Invented Christian America* (2015) is a highly-recommended eye-opener.

NO. 22

**THE ONE PERCENT**

## CEO PAY

In 2015, the average pay for an S&P CEO was $12.4 million, or 335 times the pay of a rank-and-file worker. This is an average. CEO pay was 242 times the average union worker's income, and 819 times that of a worker earning minimum wage. In 2016, CEO compensation at the largest firms was 941 percent above its 1978 level. This growth in CEO compensation far exceeded the growth of the stock market, showing that executives have done far better than the firms that they have led. Executive pay cannot be attributed to better firm performance.[62 63]

## THE 1%

Since the financial crisis of 2007–2008, the top one percent of Americans have pocketed 85 percent of total income growth. As of 2013, the average family income of the top one percent was 25 times the average income of the 99 percent. By state, the threshold to join the top one percent varies from a low of $231,276 in New Mexico to $659,979 in Connecticut. To be part of the top 0.01 percent – you needed a minimum income nationwide of $8.32 million (2013)[64]

The top one percent's share of US wealth has risen by six percentage points in the 20 years from 1992 to 2012; it is now estimated to be between 33–42 percent of total wealth. This top one percent of Americans rake in 18–23 percent of ALL income.[65]

## SPACE ALIENS

Many scientists believe we are not alone in the universe. They think it's likely that life could have arisen on at least some of the billions of planets thought to exist in our galaxy alone. In 2014, at our National Aeronautics and Space Administration (NASA), scientists convened to discuss the steps toward discovering other life in the universe. They have a plan![66]

## NO. 23
## SECOND-STORY MEN

## FINANCIAL CRIME

To see how quickly a banking system can go from stable to collapse when privatized and deregulated, watch the documentary, *Inside Job* (2010). It begins with the story of Iceland, which privatized and deregulated its banks in 2000. It took Iceland less than seven years to arrive at national bankruptcy. Three of their four major banks collapsed. (Only the bank run by women survived.) To their credit, Iceland threw 60 bankers in jail and re-nationalized their money creation. In 2007, Iceland's population was only 311,566. If we'd put the same percentage of our population in jail for banking fraud after the collapse of our economy in 2007–2008, we'd have about 600,000 new inmates. But, none of our bankers went to jail. It took our bankers the same seven short years to go from boom to bust after the 2000 deregulation of our banking and financial sectors. We bailed out our banks and gave them bonuses and presidential advisory positions instead of putting them in jail.

## COINS

Coins make up only about one percent of our total money supply. They are the *only* form of money that the US government produces, issues, and takes the *seignorage* (the difference between the cost of production and the face value when entered into the economy). In FY 2016, the US Mint shipped 16,308 million new coins. The difference between the cost of production and their face value was $579 million. The US Mint also produces gold and silver bullion and commemorative coins that earned a net of $90 million. After subtracting overall Mint operating costs, $550 million was transferred to the Treasury General Fund.[67]

NO. 24

**ABRAHAM LINCOLN AND BANKING**

## ABRAHAM LINCOLN

In the decades before the Civil War, about 1,600 state banks operated independently. About 7,000 different kinds of bank notes circulated and more than half were spurious. The Southern planters were often paid for their cotton in bills of exchange drawn on the Bank of England. The market for exchanging these bills was in the North, and the planters did not like being at the mercy of the Northern money exchangers who they considered manipulative cheats. Money was an issue that contributed to the secession of the Southern States.

When war broke out in 1861, Lincoln advocated a currency created by the private banks. He advocated for the passage of the National Banking Act, and on January 17, 1863, Lincoln argued in Congress: [that]

> *"...A uniform currency, in which taxes, subscriptions to loans and all other ordinary public dues as well as all private dues may be paid, is indispensable. Such a currency can be furnished by banking associations, organized under a general act of Congress."*

Thus Lincoln supported the banker's privilege to create money for the nation.[68]

**NO. 25**
**GREENBACKS**
- - - - - - - - - - - - -

## LEGAL TENDER

Legal tender is any medium of payment that is recognized by law, authorized by government to be used for buying, selling, repayment of debt or any financial obligation.

## GREENBACKS – CONGRESS TAKES THE INITIATIVE IN 1862

To meet the need for money to run the nation and fight the Civil War, Congressman E. G. Spaulding of Buffalo, New York introduced a bill in Congress to create legal tender commonwealth money. He justly argued that all the money in use was paper money, falsely promising to be redeemable for gold or silver. He said,

> *"… All paper currencies have been and ever will be irredeemable. It is a pleasant fiction to call them redeemable…I would not expose that fiction only that the great emergency which is upon us seems to me to render it more than usually proper that the nation should begin to speak the truth to itself; to have done with shams, and to deal with realities." This sounds like good advice for today, too.*

Spaulding's argument won and The Legal Tender Law was passed in 1862, authorizing the issuance of what came to be called, *Greenbacks*. The Greenbacks were not a promise to pay *money* later. They were themselves money, guaranteed by the full faith, credit and commonwealth of the nation. There was no interest due on this money as it had not been borrowed from a bank creating money for the nation. Congress authorized the issuance of $450 million in Greenbacks, and did not exceed this mandate.

The Greenbacks got the nation through the war. After the war, the bankers marshalled against them, and got the National Banking Act of 1863/64 passed. This put the power to create money back into the hands of the private banking sector.[69]

**NO. 26**

**LUCKY STRIKE**

## GAMBLING

In 2014, Americans spent $70 billion on lottery tickets. That's more than the total spending on music, books, sports teams, movies and video games combined, according to CNN Money. The $70 billion Americans spend on lottery tickets translates into roughly $230 per person, including children, per year. That's a lot of money not being saved for retirement or used to pay off credit card debt or used to buy better food, safer housing or education. It's also *"more than 10% of the total state revenue in states' collective budgets for fiscal year 2014,"* according to the Pew Charitable Trusts. According to Reuters, *"the 44 states with lotteries (plus the District of Columbia and Puerto Rico) get 44 cents from this form of gambling for each dollar of state corporate income tax."* At last count, there were 11 states in which lottery revenues exceeded revenues from corporate taxes. And most lottery gamblers are poor. My home state of Oregon draws about 5.5 percent of its revenue from gambling. There is something deeply immature and warped about gathering revenue for basic commonwealth services by suckering mostly the poor into gambling.

## no. 27
## FOX AND HENS

## WHO CREATES OUR MONEY?

The *1863–1864 National Banking Act* provided for the national chartering of banks who in addition to providing banking services (storage, transfer, accounting) would have the power to create a national legal tender money for the nation. This Act mostly eliminated the power of Congress to create money; if Congress needed money, it would have to borrow from the bankers and pay them interest. This Act established rules and regulations that cleaned up some of the operational fraud that had been rampant. However, the National Banking Act entrenched the power of bankers to create money mostly unfettered, and to charge interest on the money they create for the nation. After a short period of rapid expansion of the money supply, the Great Depression of 1873–1896 followed, then panics in 1901 and 1907.

Intending to create a more stable currency, Congress passed the *Federal Reserve Act of 1913*. This Act left the power to create money in the hands of the private bankers, but established a government-authorized and guaranteed central bank to serve the bankers with backup money creation power. (If an individual bank messed up, they could borrow from each other through the central bank, or the central bank could create some new money for them by lending to them.) Another short period of rapid expansion of the money supply and a Gilded Age for those with the power to create money was again followed by a depression in 1920–21, and then the Wall Street Crash of 1929 and the Great Depression. The 20[TH] century saw an expansion and contraction of the money supply every 8–12 years.

## no. 28
## SELLING SEX
- - - - - - - - - - - - -

## SEX TRAFFICKING IN AMERICA

The Department of Homeland Security defines human trafficking as a *"modern-day form of slavery involving the illegal trade of people for exploitation or commercial gain."* In the US in 2014, four thousand cases of sex trafficking were reported – these are women and girls forced into commercial sex. Since the victims are generally effectively silenced, the number is likely far higher.

The International Labour Organization (ILO), in a 2014 report on global *Profits and Poverty: The Economics of Forced Labour,* estimates that roughly $100 billion in profits are made on the sexual exploitation of women and girls. On average, the exploiter makes a profit of $21,800 per girl per year."[70][71][72]

**NO. 29**
## GRANTING PRIVILEGE

## ULYSSES S. GRANT

Our 18ᵀᴴ US President and famous Civil War general, Ulysses S. Grant appeared on the $50 bill in 1913.

In 1868, Grant was elected president in the middle of a hotly contested argument over how the US money system should work. Greenbacks, the official currency of the US, had been issued since 1862 by legislative authorization rather than the caprice of bankers. They were legal tender created by and guaranteed by the commonwealth of the United States. Keeping Greenbacks as our money was very popular among Americans and very unpopular among bankers. Bankers lobbied hard to return to a money system that allowed them to control the economy and create the nation's money. Requiring that the Greenback notes be convertible into gold was one way for the bankers to take back power.

The Democratic Party and their candidate, Horatio Seymour supported the continuing use of the Greenbacks. The Republican Party and their candidate, Ulysses S. Grant, favored the bankers. Grant won and his first act on taking office in March 1869 was an act pledging to redeem government bonds in gold rather than Greenbacks, which effectively killed the popular Greenbacks and set the stage for a return to banker created money.

Again, if you love history, Stephen Zarlenga's *Lost Science of Money* (2002) is a rich trove of stories.

NO. 30

**PLAYING THE GAME**

## US ENTERTAINMENT

Americans spend roughly five percent of our household budget on entertainment. This holds true even during recessions and depressions, and across all income levels. Mean annual entertainment expenditures range from 4.3 percent for people in the second lowest 20ᵀᴴ percentile to 5.2 percent for the 20 percent with the highest incomes. Here's how we spend that 5 percent:

- 1.1%  on fees and admissions,
- 1.9%  on audio and visual equipment and services,
- 1.2%  on pets, toys, and playground equipment,
- 0.7%  on other entertainment. [73]

## FREE LUNCH – RUNNING AWAY WITH THE DISH AND THE SPOON

In 2015, the National Football League (NFL) took in $13 billion – about half from TV deals. On the TV deals alone each NFL team got $226.4 million, allowing them to pay average salaries of $1.9 million (rookies average $365,000 and the highest paid earn salaries over $24 million).

In 2015, Forbes valued NFL franchises from $1.5 billion for the Bills to $4.2 billion for the Cowboys (who made an estimated $700 million in 2015). However, while the teams rake in big bucks, their stadiums, facilities, and property bills are often footed by taxpayers, with little revenue actually returning to the community. Between 2001 and 2010 a whopping $12 billion in public funds went for 51 new sports facilities around the country. In Wisconsin, Governor Scott Walker (R) cut $250 million from universities to pay for half the cost of the new Milwaukee Bucks arena. The City of Detroit, just six days after filing for bankruptcy, committed to paying $283 million for a new stadium for the Redwings, owned by Mike Ilitch (1929–2017) founder of Little Caesars Pizza, whose estimated net worth was $5.1 billion. Is this the best use of taxpayer money?[74] [75] [76] [77] [78]

## NO. 31
## CROCODILE SWAMP

## CROCODILE SWAMP

The Environmental Protection Agency classes Koch industries as the largest producers of toxic waste in the country and one of the largest air polluters, climate polluters and water polluters. Some of the biggest legal cases against polluting industries are against Koch Industries. According to an economic curriculum they have funded and sponsored, *Common Sense Economics*, it's OK to kill a few employees or consumers, if it makes a bigger profit. They have used their fortunes to put this curriculum in high schools and universities across our nation.

Here is one selection from the Common Sense Economics website: *"Sacrificing Lives for Profits,"* by Common Sense Economics co-author Dwight Lee. It argues we'd all be better off if companies cut corners, even risking customers' lives, in the name of profit. He says,

> *The charge that sways juries and offends public sensitivities ... is that greedy corporations sacrifice human lives to increase their profits. Is this charge true? Of course it is. But this isn't a criticism of corporations; rather it is a reflection of the proper functioning of a market economy. Corporations routinely sacrifice the lives of some of their customers to increase profits, and we are all better off because they do. That's right, we are lucky to live in an economy that allows corporations to increase profits by intentionally selling products less safe than could be produced. The desirability of sacrificing lives for profits may not be as comforting as milk, cookies and a bedtime story, but it follows directly from a reality we cannot wish away. The reality is scarcity.*[79]

Back in 1980 David Koch was the VP candidate on the Libertarian ticket, which got 1.06 percent of the vote. Discouraged by these election results, David Koch switched his efforts and vast fortune to buying think tanks, 'grassroots' organizations, and university chairs and departments to promote his ideas. Please read Jane Mayer's book, *Dark Money* (2017). It is a critical read for understanding how we got where we are today with the power of a very few controlling our entire economy for their personal benefit – at the cost of lives, and the cost of a sustainable life of this planet.

**NO. 32**
**NEST EGG**

## NEST EGGS

People think deposits and savings are required for loans, and savings limit the amount of money the private banking system is able to loan out. Neither is true.

When people save for their future, savings get them through emergencies, or they can lend or invest. But, *banks* do not need savings to create new money. And when they use savings for their lending they have to pay a percentage to the saver, which cuts into their profits. So, the amount of money people save has been slowly shrinking. The FED reports, *"In the past two decades, the… personal saving rate for the United States has been trending down, dropping from averages of around 9 percent in the 1980s, to approximately 5 percent in the 1990s, to almost zero in the first years of the new century."* In fact, we have been recording negative savings rates in many quarters for the last decade, which means people are taking more out of savings than is going in. Some of this is due to retiring boomers drawing on their savings, but given the numbers, there should be a balance of young savers and there isn't. (Increasing student debt is a factor.) In June 2017 the national personal savings rate is at 3.8 percent.

Big business has been doing the same. They spend more buying their own stock than they save and invest in capital improvements – and often more than they pay out in dividends. Buying their own stock juices its value, so the business has greater borrowing power and CEOs can collect higher compensation (which is often over 80% based on stock values).

According to the FED's accounts, during the 20 years from 1981–2000, corporations spent $540 billion more buying their own stock back than they sold in stock to new investors. Between 2003 and 2013 the S&P 500 companies used 54 percent of their earnings – a total of $2.4 trillion – to buy back their own stock, pumping up the market price of shares. By 2014, the annual amount spent on buybacks was over $540 billion. The dearth of long-term investment ultimately hollows out the business. When individuals and businesses have no savings upon which to draw for big investments or to cover unforeseen calamities, they must borrow. Since our current money system demands increasing amounts of borrowing, the bankers are happy.[80][81][82]

**NO. 33**
**SPIN GREEN**

## DEFORESTATION

Trees are critical to survival. They take the air animals breath out and turn it into the oxygen we breathe in. They convert not only the air we breathe out, but they act as a carbon sink, soaking up the excess man-made greenhouse gases that fuel global warming. Fewer forests means more global warming.

About 80 percent of the Earth's land animals live in forests and deforestation destroys their homes, causing the die off of entire species. Forests of trees also help keep the water cycle turning — absorbing water that falls, storing it, and returning water vapor to the atmosphere. Without trees, land can become a barren desert. Trees keep the climate more temperate; they keep the ground cooler by blocking the sun's rays during the day, and hold in heat at night.

We have removed 90 percent of the forests that were present in the continental US in 1600. Forests still cover about 30% of Earth's landmasses. However, we are losing the equivalent of some 48 football fields every MINUTE — some 46–58 thousand square miles of forest are lost each year. This is not sustainable.[83][84]

## NO. 34 AND 35
## BEN'S BALLS

## BEN FRANKLIN AND THE MONEY POWER

The Colonies in pre-Revolutionary America were hotbeds of money system experimentation. Many of the colonies experimented with creating, authorizing and guaranteeing their own money with the full faith, credit and commonwealth of their Colony. For example, in 1690 Massachusetts issued Bills of Credit, that were a promise made by the government to accept these bills for all money due to Massachusetts. They spent these bills into circulation. These notes were sovereign-commonwealth money, in that they were authorized by government and legal tender; they were backed only by the full faith, credit and commonwealth of the colony; they could not be converted into anything else (as with a gold-backed currency); and, they were created by the Colony's legislative assembly.

The Colony of Pennsylvania in the 1720s created a sovereign-commonwealth money they loaned into circulation against the assets of borrowers. This was money created and authorized by government as legal tender. It was backed by the full faith and credit of the colony and whatever the borrowers put up as collateral. This money was so successful, an admiring Benjamin Franklin wrote a pamphlet titled, *A Modest Inquiry into the Nature and Necessity of Paper Currency* (1729).[85]

## NO. 36
## LIONS AND TIGERS AND BEARS

## THE LION ROARED

To fund our nation's Revolutionary War, our Congress twice issued $200 million in citizen money, *Continentals*, for a total of $400 million. Continentals were issued by the Revolutionary government and guaranteed by the full faith, credit and commonwealth of our new nation. Our Congress issued a reasoned and reasonable amount. This money carried the new country through five and a half years of warfare. Without our own currency, we could not have won the Revolutionary War.

However, the private global banking cartels did not want a new nation with its own sovereign currency and issued millions of counterfeit Continentals. At one point in the war, the British had a ship moored off our eastern coast with a printing press on board churning out counterfeit money, intending to crash our currency and win and crush the revolution. We won the war for independence, but the excessive counterfeiting by the British and the bankers caused inflation, and doubt about the authenticity and value of the Continental bills. The global bankers over the following decades turned the lion into a docile cat.

## THREE BLIND MICE

It's difficult to follow the debates about money that have been ongoing for millennia. It's clear in US history that many people with the power to make decisions did not really understand what money is or how it works – as is true today. There are at least five basic kinds of money, with variations of each kind. People mix up discussions of kinds of money with economic theories and with theories of governance. I've done my best in my book, *US Money: Piecing Together a Better Alternative* (2018), to explain the different kinds of money, so that it is easier to have a useful discussion of options. Let me know how I did at **USmoney.US**.

## NO. 37
## TIME CAGE

## WAGE EARNERS

Productivity in the US has surged since 1970, but income and wages have stagnated for most Americans. If the median household income had kept pace with the economy since 1970, it would now be nearly $92,000, not $50,000.[86]

## MINIMUM WAGE

In 2016, 80 million workers age 16 and older were paid at hourly rates. This represents 59 percent of all wage and salary workers. Of these hourly workers, 2.2 million were paid at or below the minimum wage of $7.25 per hour.

About half of minimum wage workers are under age 25. Obviously, the other half are over 25 and more likely to have families to support.[87]

The increase in the real value of the minimum wage has only gone up 21% since 1990, but in that same time from, the cost of living has increased 67%. Someone working for minimum wage only makes $15,080 per year. A single worker requires at least $30,000 to have real economic security.

There is no State in the Union where these workers can find an affordable place to live (2-bedrooms costing no more than 1/3 of their income). In Hawaii, our most expensive housing state, a breadwinner would have to work 175 hours/week at minimum wage to afford basic housing. That's not even possible; there are only 168 hours in a week – 24/7! In America nearly one in four working families spend more than half of their income on housing. They short other basics like health care and food. The stress of multiple jobs and juggling bills is a killer.[88] [89] [90]

## NO. 38
## WORKER BEE

## WORKER UNIONS

The labor movement in the US fought for better wages, reasonable hours and safer working conditions. Their efforts stopped child labor, brought us the 40-hour workweek and weekends, gave many workers health benefits, and established some provisions for injured and retired workers. A union can balance the power and interests of owners and employees.

In 1983, union membership rate was 20 percent. In 2016 it was down to 10.7 percent.

In 2016, the median yearly earnings of union workers were $52,208. Non-union workers' median yearly earnings were $41,704.

Germany presents an interesting and successful model of a new economy. They have muscular unions. In fact, businesses are required by law to include worker representation on their boards. *And*, they push for corporate efficiency and profits. They have high-cost workers with generous benefits who successfully compete in global manufacturing. They have low levels of unemployment and a base of independent small and medium manufacturers able to compete on the highest levels of productivity and efficiency. It is a model of capitalism at least worth studying, if not emulating.[91][92]

**NO. 39**

**SHIP OF HOPE**

## NASA

The National Aeronautics and space Administration (NASA) began operation on October 1, 1958. It had about 8,000 employees and an annual budget of $100 million, which was about 0.1 percent of the federal budget. During the Space Race of the 1960s – catching up with and surpassing Russia, the first nation to put a satellite in space – the NASA budget rose to a peak of 4.41% of the federal budget in 1966. The United States was putting satellites into the sky and sending men to the moon. After this peak, the money we allotted to scientific research and space slowly declined, dropping about one tenth of one percent each year, until it reached about half of one percent in 2010, where it has remained. In 2017, NASA's budget is $19.6 billion which represents about 0.5 percent of the $3.4 trillion US federal budget. NASA spending also represents about 35 percent of total spending on academic scientific research in the United States.

Many NASA technologies, developed in its research have become invisible yet critical aspects of our daily activities and well-being. Light-Emitting Diodes (LEDs); Infrared ear thermometers; artificial limbs; ventricular assist devices that function as a bridge to heart transplants; anti-icing systems for aircraft; safety grooving in concrete; chemical detectors; video enhancing and analysis systems; land mine removal technologies; fire-resistant reinforcement shielding; firefighter gear; temper foam; enriched baby food; portable cordless vacuums; freeze drying technology; solar energy technologies; pollution remediation; software improvements for real-time weather visualization and forecasting, high-resolution 3-D maps; refrigerated internet-connected wall ovens; powdered lubricants; improved mine safety; food safety systems; and, more. We have made a significant return on our investment.[93]

NO. 40
DIGITAL SWAMP

## WHO LEGALLY OWNS YOUR FACEBOOK POSTS?

If you post something to Facebook using the *"Public"* setting, while Facebook says that you *"own"* your posts, anyone can use your information. For example, you can post a photo or video that you have copyrighted. But, according to Findlaw.com (2014), Facebook's terms allow them *"a non-exclusive, transferable, sub-licensable, royalty-free, worldwide license to use any IP content that you post on or in connection with Facebook."* As they note, *"In layman's terms, Facebook has license to use the photos and videos you post (which you own) in any way it sees fit, without paying you, and it can transfer that license to third parties."* [94]

## WHO OWNS YOUR SEARCH ENGINE HISTORY?

Currently whoever provides your broadband can track you, and sell that data, unless you individually opt out. Our Federal Communications Commission (FCC) has privacy rules for phones and cable television, but they do not apply to internet service providers (ISPs). The FCC noted under President Obama, *"Your web browser contains a treasure trove of data, including your health concerns, shopping habits...where you bank, your political views and sexual orientation."* To address this, Obama's FCC proposed protections that would require ISPs get your consent before they sold your web browsing patterns. The new rules were called the Broadband Consumer Privacy Proposal and were due to apply as early as December 2017.

On March 28, 2017 a Republican majority in the US House of Representatives passed S.J. Resolution 34 that overturns these protections (Yeas: 215 Republicans, Nays 190 Democrats and 15 Republicans). This resolution became public law on April 4, 2017. ISPs like Comcast, AT&T and Verizon *can* sell your web browsing histories directly to marketers, financial firms and other companies without your consent. The Resolution also bans the FCC from issuing rules similar to the Obama protections in the future.[95] [96]

**NO. 41**
**NINJAS**

## NINJA LOANS

*Subprime* loans are loans made to people with poor to middling credit. They cost the borrower more to borrow and interest rates are higher. But they can mean higher profits for loan initiators, especially if they can pass the higher risk on to others. Before 2003, subprime mortgages were 2–3 percent of total mortgages. Financial deregulation in 2000 sent the percentage soaring to about 11 percent in 2003, and then up to 14 percent by 2007. One form of subprime loan became notorious prior to the 2007–2008 market crash. The NINJA loan was so named because one could get the loan with **N**o Income, **N**o **J**ob or **A**ssets.

Many of these loans were Adjustable Rate Mortgages (ARMS). One might start out with a low interest rate, but the rate could change substantially. In California in 2005, 34% of all new mortgages were interest only for the first few years. NINJA and ARM loans set many people up to fail. Some people borrowed substantial amounts – sometimes right up to the full bubble market value of their home, because they could afford the early years' low interest-only payments. When the payments jumped up to include principle, and the interest went up, and the market crash brought the value of their homes down, they were underwater (their home was worth less than they owed on it).[97] [98]

## no. 42
## FREE SHEEP

## BAA BAA BLACK SHEEP

People will agree with others, even when their eyes, ears, or minds tell them the others are wrong. The Asch Conformity experiments developed in the 1950s (and still used today) use seven confederates and one subject all sitting in a row looking at a series of boards with two vertical lines of varying lengths. Each person in the row is asked which of two lines is longer. When the first seven people – confederates of the experimenter who are instructed to give wrong answers – give the clearly wrong answer, the subject struggles but more often than not agrees with the people who had gone before, even though their answer is obviously wrong. About 65 percent of the subjects agreed with the others rather than stand alone in dissent.

However, when only one other person gave the correct answer, many more subjects also stated the correct answer. This is why it is important to speak up when you think someone is making an incorrect assessment or choice. One person speaking up often represents others who agree, but hesitate to say so.

When we recognize this tendency toward groupthink, we can take steps to assure we have independence and diversity in all our community decision-making bodies – at local, state and federal levels. Only in diversity will we have our assumptions challenged and the widest selection of constructive options available.

For an explanation of why the best decisions are made by a diverse group of informed and independent thinkers (the founding principle of a democratic republic), I highly recommend James Suroweicki's book, *The Wisdom of Crowds: Why the Many Are Smarter Than the Few and How Collective Wisdom Shapes Business, Economies, Societies and Nations* (2004).[99]

**NO. 43**

**THE GRINCH STOLE DADDY**

## ON KILLING

Lt. Col. Dave Grossman wrote an interesting book called, *On Killing; The Psychological Cost of Learning to Kill in War and Society* (1995). Military historians have added up the number of guns, soldiers, bullets used, and deaths, and found that up through WWII, there was a very low kill rate. Brigadier General S.L.A. Marshall, who studied wars up through WWII, found that historically and consistently, the vast majority of combat veterans simply would not kill in war – over 80 percent!

The military considered this low kill rate to be costly and inefficient, and it has spent decades discovering how to desensitize and condition our soldiers (and police) to be better and more efficient killers – no pointing and firing away from a subject, no wasting bullets. They have succeeded and the kill ratio is above the 90th percentile. But, there is a price to pay. About 98 percent of humans are not natural born killers; we can be trained to be killers, but when we are, post-traumatic stress disorders (PTSD) increase substantially.

According to the National Center for PTSD at the Veterans Affairs, about 11–20 percent of veterans from Operations Iraqi Freedom have PTSD in a given year. About 12 percent of Gulf War veterans have PTSD in a given year. About 30% of Vietnam Veterans have had PTSD in their lifetime. In 2009 the suicide rate in the US population among males was 19.4 and females, 4.9 per 100,000. In the same year, the rate for male veterans was 38.3 per 100,000, and for female veterans 12.8 per 100,000. If you just count young men, close to their military service, The LA Times estimates that roughly 1.5 veterans commit suicide every day. If you include all veterans of all ages, who may be decades away from their service, about 22 commit suicide every day.[100] [101] [102]

## NO. 44
## CRIME AND PUNISHMENT?

## THE UNITED STATES SECRET SERVICE

The US Secret Service is part of the Treasury Department, reflecting its role as protector of our currency. On their website, they say, *"The United States Secret Service is one of the oldest federal law enforcement agencies in the country and ranks among the most elite in the world. With its origin dating back to the end of the American Civil War (1865), the Secret Service was originally founded to combat the then-widespread counterfeiting of US currency... In 1867, the Secret Service responsibilities broadened to include 'detecting persons perpetrating frauds against the government.' In 1901, the agency was asked to begin its protective mission after the assassination of President William McKinley – the third sitting US President to be assassinated. Today, the Secret Service proudly continues to protect both national leaders and visiting foreign dignitaries while helping to secure the nation's financial infrastructure through financial and cybercrime investigations."* [103]

## WHITE-COLLAR CRIME

Sociologist Edwin Sutherland was the first to define white-collar crime as *"a crime committed by a person of respectability and high social status in the course of his occupation."* Today, it generally refers to financially motivated nonviolent crime committed by business and government professionals. [104]

## SHOPLIFTING AND EMPLOYEE THEFT

Shoplifting and employee theft cost US retail stores nearly $48.9 billion in 2016. That sounds like a lot, but it is an average inventory shrink rate of 1.44 percent, which isn't doing too badly. Of that total, shoplifting accounts for 37 percent, employees steal 30 percent, administrative errors account for 21 percent, and vendor fraud for 5 percent. [105]

NO. 45

**COMMONWEALTH MONEY**

## THE ELUSIVE SPONDULIX

My friend Vicki's mother used to refer to money as the elusive *sponduli*. It's such a fun name we looked it up. It appears to have entered the English language from American slang of the 1800s. African and West Indies cowry shell money, called *spondu*, was on display at the Philadelphia Mint. Corrupted a bit, as happens with slang, it became *sponduli* or *spondulix*. W.C. Field may have originated the phrase, the elusive spondulix.

*"Have you any of the elusive spondulix on you?"*
W.C. Fields in<br>My Little Chickadee, 1940

## COMMONWEALTH MONEY

I hope you will read my book, *US Money: Piecing Together a Better Alternative* (2018). It explains our current money system, the consequences, and makes a case for switching to commonwealth money. When we change from a private banker money creation system to a commonwealth money system, prices will be lower, there will be less debt, taxes can be reduced, and we can be happier and healthier. Changing systems can be done overnight with an accounting change. Find out why and how!

There are growing movements globally to switch from private banker money to commonwealth-citizen money. In the United States, **The American Monetary Institute,** monetary.org, has been at the vanguard. **The Public Banking Institute**, publicbankinginstitute.org, offers a *partial* step toward citizen money.

In Great Britain, **Positive Money**, positivemoney.org has developed an enthusiastic following with a well-crafted website and a collection of great videos explaining money.

**The International Movement for Monetary Reform**, Internationalmoneyreform.org has links to commonwealth money movements in Australia, Bulgaria, Croatia, Denmark, Finland, France, Germany, Greece, India, Iceland, Ireland, Israel, The Netherlands, Poland, Portugal, Puerto Rico, Slovakia, South Africa, Spain, Sweden, and Switzerland.

**no. 46**

**JOB LUCK**

## LUCK

The Atlantic reports,

*"Chance plays a far larger role in life outcomes than most people realize. And yet, the luckiest among us appear especially unlikely to appreciate our good fortune. According to the Pew Research Center, people in higher income brackets are much more likely than those with lower incomes to say that individuals get rich primarily because they work hard. Other surveys bear this out: Wealthy people overwhelmingly attribute their own success to hard work rather than to factors like luck or being in the right place at the right time. That's troubling, because a growing body of evidence suggest that seeing ourselves as self-made — rather than as talented, hardworking, and lucky — leads us to be less generous and public spirited. It may even make the lucky less likely to support the conditions (such as high-quality public infrastructure and education) that made their own success possible."* [106]

## THE GREAT SEAL

Charles Thomson, a prominent Philadelphia merchant and secretary of the Continental Congress presented the Great Seal of the United States to Congress in 1782. Charles Thomson explained that *"an American Eagle on the wing and rising"* was chosen because it flies freely, independent of any support. The Eagle holds 13 arrows, signifying war in its left talon, and an olive branch, signifying peace, in its right. The hand matters. The right hand is considered dominant, and when the eagles on the backs of our silver coins from 1801 to 1807 switched the hands, some European journalists and diplomats considered this an aggressive gesture and grounds for promoting war. The design was changed back in 1807. Across the eagle are the words, *"E Pluribus Unum,"* which Thomson translates to mean *"Out of many, one."*

The unfinished pyramid on the other side was to signify *"strength and duration."* Composed of 13 rows of building blocks representing the original colonies, Roman numerals on the bottom row read 1776. Thomson wanted to signify *"the beginning of the new American Era."* Inspired by Virgil, he composed a motto in Latin, *"Novus Ordo Seclorum,"* which translates to *"A New order of the Ages."* The Latin motto above the eye, *"Annuit Coeptis"* translates to *"Providence Has Favored Our Undertakings."* [107]

**NO. 47**
**SPIN GOLD**

## DIGITAL MONEY

Currently about 97 percent of all the money in use today is an accounting record, and about 95 percent is a digital record — created with a few key strokes made by a bank, and then transferred around and around in our economy by digital means.

## CRYPTO-CURRENCY

A crypto-currency is a kind of digital currency that uses cryptography to secure transactions and to control the creation of additional units of currency. Bitcoin, a curious experiment in a private, self-regulated, global currency, became the first decentralized cryptocurrency in 2009. It modeled itself on gold money, calling itself a *coin*, and calling the computer wizards who performed tasks that brought new money into creation, *miners*. It is designed to reach a fixed limit of coins — 21 million. It is not designed to be a currency with a stable value; it is designed to be an increasing value currency. This makes it do double duty: as a collectible asset with a fluctuating value and as a medium of exchange. Any time a currency is serving this dual duty, it can be manipulated by those with great wealth.

## BLOCKCHAIN TECHNOLOGY

Bitcoin was introduced as a distributed platform, which means the whole program resides on many computers. This distribution functions as a backup system assuring a level of trustworthiness. If one computer fails, the entire program and its data resides on many other platforms. The code that creates a Bitcoin consists of chains of information, called blockchain technology. Each digital coin carries its full creation and transfer history as little blocks of information and this information resides on many computers. A counterfeiter would face the nearly impossible task of altering information in a chain of information that resides on many computers. Some are calling blockchain technology one of the most important innovations in computer coding in a generation. It is being researched and adopted by banks globally for transferring money securely. And, venture capital funds are investing billions to make fortunes with its next best use.[108]

**NO. 48**
**BE WORKER BEE**

## WHOEVER HAS THE POWER TO CREATE MONEY RULES

Money *creation* is not when you build a business and make lots of money; money creation is when you increase the supply of money in use. Today private bankers create over 97 percent of US money. When private bankers create a nations money by lending they choose how the nation invests for the future, what new ideas are developed, who gets to borrow and benefit. This gives them the power to control who governs and the decisions our government at all levels makes. When we gave private bankers the power to create our money, we gave them sovereign power over the country. Over the past century, wealth has been shifting into the hands of this very wealthy few, who are buying up our natural resources, real property, municipal revenue sources, privately held wealth and the commonwealth. [109]

**NO. 49**
**GRASS ROOTS**

## CANNABIS – HEMP – MARIJUANA – GRASS

Cannabis is a genus of flowering plant with several species. Various species have been used for millennia for fiber, oils, medicinal, recreational and spiritual purposes. By 2006, Marijuana was the largest cash crop in the US, more valuable than corn and wheat combined. Conservative estimates valued domestic marijuana production at over $35 billion. Despite many efforts to eradicate domestic marijuana, the production increased ten-fold in the 25 years from 1980 to 2005 – from 1,000 metric tons (2.2 million pounds) in 1981 to 10,000 metric tons (22 million pounds) in 2006. Since 1973, US states have been slowly decriminalizing cannabis – first for medicinal uses, then in small quantities for recreational use, and then open recreational use. Oregon legalized recreational cannabis in 2014. In 2017, Oregon estimates that the recreational and medical marijuana industry has created 12,500 jobs, with cumulative annual wages of $315 million.[110] [111]

## GRASSROOTS

I'm a dedicated quilter and civic advocate on a mission: to educate and facilitate a discussion about our current money system, its consequences, an alternative, and why it is important to change it. This is a call-out to quilters.

The 2014 Quilting in America Survey found that 10.3 percent of US households (12.62 million) are home to at least one active quilter. The estimated total dollar value of the quilting industry is $3.76 billion. In the US there are 16.4 million quilters and 12 percent are *dedicated* quilters – two million of us! We are people who spend more than $500 per year on quilting related purchases, tend to be female, 64 years old, well-educated (79 percent attended college), affluent ($101,080 average household income), have been quilting for an average of 20.3 years and spend on average $3,296 per year on quilting. We have time, we have energy, we have power. Let's use it to make our economy sustainable and prosperous by learning about and improving our money system. Please help me make the mission a reality by buying my book *US Money: Piecing Together a Better Alternative* (2018) . It's about the money system, illustrated with quilts and published in January 2018. And/or, go to **USmoney.US** to read it, discuss and comment on its contents.[112]

Salonpas
Pain Relieving Patch
Stiff Neck • Sore Shoulder
Backache • Joint Pain
Paper Pieces
La Passacaglia
Piece E
1368 Pieces
ThimblePad
John James

## TOOLS AND SUPPLIES

If you enjoy handwork, you will enjoy English Paper Piecing. Everything you need is easy to cart around and work on here or there. I confess I watched a lot of TV shows where I could follow the plot without watching the screen attentively. PBS dramas don't work so well.

**TEMPLATES AND MATCHING PAPERS.** There are many posts online about making or printing your own. I consider it well worth the time savings to buy the templates and papers from *PaperPieces.com*. I bought the complete Passacaglia set of templates and papers, and enough individual packages to complete another 11 wheels.

**DESIGN BOARDS.** I have two 4' x 8' *Insulfoam R-Tec* insulation pieces that I have covered with white fleece for my design boards. In the auditioning stages, nearly all the pins you see here were in use.

**NEEDLES, THREAD AND PINS.** I used size 11 John James Quilting needles. I experimented with a number of threads and found I liked the *Bottom Line*, 60 wt. polyester from *Superior Threads by Libby Lehman*. I started out with a ring of bobbins they sell, and then bought full size spools of the ones I used most. I used a Clover Wonder Clip to hold the pieces in place when I started a seam.

**MORE.** I only use the Olfa deluxe rotary cutter, because it covers the blade when you set it down. There is no chance of bumping into an exposed blade — one of those hard lessons.

I used *Sewline Fabric Glue* pen and a gazillion refills to glue baste the papers to the fabric (instead of sew basting them). This cost adds up, and again, there are posts online about how to economize successfully. It was worth my time to find them on sale and stock up. I used a *Violet Craft Seam Roller* to get a sharp edge on the pieces after glue basting.

In the *"I couldn't have done it without"* category: *Thimblepads* saved my fingers. I've never been able to use a thimble and I've tried many kinds. *Thimblepads* work great for me; they don't get in the way and they protect my fingertips. *Salonpas* were a lifesaver. I have the beginnings of arthritic knuckles, and putting these little patches on overnight mostly eliminated any pain. They were indispensable.

**FABRICS.** This quilt took more fabric than any quilt I have ever made. It can take several yards to fussy cut up to 20 shapes, so I have lots of fabric with many holes. Nearly all the fabrics I used were quilters' cottons. I found that the fabrics with the older style metallic ink were a little harder on the fingers (but, worth it!). I am especially grateful to my home fabric stores, *The Pine Needle* in Lake Oswego, Oregon, and the incomparable *Fabric Depot* in Portland. Portland, Oregon is a quilter's paradise, and I also found fabrics at many of our wonderful and unique quilt shops – A Common Thread, Cool Cottons, Modern Domestic, Pioneer Quilts, Quilter's Corner, Mill End Store, Hollyhill Quilt Shoppe, Craft Warehouse, and worth a venture into Washington state, Country Manor. I found many fabrics online – especially when I was looking for a fabric with a specific image, and I ordered and created several fabrics on Spoonflower.

What a world we live in! I am so grateful for all the shortcuts offered in our marketplace, and how widely one can wander to find special treasures. May the wheels continue to turn!

I've blogged about the process of making this quilt at **PieceItTogether.org.** Come visit and sign up for updates about my quilting. Thank you reading through to the end.

With my warmest wishes,

Virginia Hammon

Lewis Pera helping with the binding

# ENDNOTES

1. This is a story that first began circulating after the Great Depression. It may have been around long before. I do not know who first told it.
2. (These were all online last year. When I went to double check on the link I had used they were gone. It may take time to find them again, so please check my website USMONEY.US for an update.)
3. http://www.businessinsider.com/happiness-benchmark-for-annual-income-2014-7
4. http://prosperityuk.com/2001/01/a-wonderful-wizard-of-oz-a-monetary-reform-parable/
5. https://www.ers.usda.gov/amber-waves/2016/september/percent-of-income-spent-on-food-falls-as-income-rises/
6. https://www.oxfam.org/en/press-room/pressreleases/2017-01-16/just-8-men-own-same-wealth-half-world
7. https://www.fastcompany.com/3061516/scientific-proof-that-buying-things-can-actually-buy-happiness-sometimes
8. http://www.audubon.org/news/thirty-percent-north-american-bird-species-face-decline-across-seasons
9. http://www.iata.org/pressroom/facts_figures/fact_sheets/Documents/fact-sheet-industry-facts.pdf
10. https://www.allianz.com/v_1474281539000/media/economic_research/publications/specials/en/AGWR2016e.pdf
11. https://www.thenation.com/article/20-people-now-own-as-much-wealth-as-half-of-all-americans/
12. http://fortune.com/2015/09/30/america-wealth-inequality/
13. https://venturebeat.com/2015/04/22/video-games-will-make-91-5b-this-year/
14. http://pediatrics.aappublications.org/content/pediatrics/early/2014/07/29/peds.2013-4021.full.pdf
15. http://www.pewresearch.org/fact-tank/2016/09/07/some-americans-dont-use-the-internet-who-are-they/
16. https://www.wired.com/1999/10/ports/
17. http://www.prb.org/publications/datasheets/2012/world-population-data-sheet/fact-sheet-us-population.aspx
18. http://www.migrationpolicy.org/programs/data-hub/charts/immigrant-population-over-time
19. http://www.nytimes.com/2011/07/05/health/05social.html
20. https://www.si.edu/Encyclopedia_SI/nmnh/buginfo/bugnos.htm
21. https://extension.entm.purdue.edu/radicalbugs/default.php?page=importance_of_insects
22. http://www.overshootday.org/about-earth-overshoot-day/national-ecological-deficit-days/
23. http://historymatters.gmu.edu/d/5354/
24. http://www.taxpolicycenter.org/statistics/historical-highest-marginal-income-tax-rates
25. https://www.scientificamerican.com/article/only-60-years-of-farming-left-if-soil-degradation-continues/

26 https://www.ers.usda.gov/data.../ag-and.../ag-and-food-sectors-and-the-economy.aspx
27 USmoney.Us
28 https://www.bls.gov/news.release/laus.nr0.htm
29 http://www.dailymail.co.uk/news/article-2730947/Americans-paid-vacation-time-world-countries-enjoy-FORTY-days-year.html
30 https://www.inc.com/jayson-demers/how-much-time-do-your-employees-waste-at-work-each-day.html
31 http://ngm.nationalgeographic.com/2011/07/food-ark/food-variety-graphic
32 https://www.census.gov/quickfacts/fact/table/US/PST045216
33 https://rodaleinstitute.org/chemical-cotton/
34 https://www.nwf.org/News-and-Magazines/National-Wildlife/Green-Living/Archives/2006/Cotton-and-Pesticides.aspx
35 http://www.crimescene-forensics.com/History_of_Fingerprints.html
36 http://www.slate.com/articles/news_and_politics/explainer/2005/04/does_the_fbi_have_your_fingerprints.html
37 https://en.wikipedia.org/wiki/Salmon_P._Chase
38 https://www.powerofpositivity.com/the-bee-population-is-resurging-in-europe-heres-why/
39 https://www.bls.gov/cpi/N0.data
40 http://www.shadowstats.com/article/no-438-public-comment-on-inflation-measurement
41 https://www.cbsnews.com/news/for-a-longer-life-researchers-say-eat-this-many-fruits-and-veggies-per-day/
42 https://www.theguardian.com/lifeandstyle/2003/may/10/foodanddrink.shopping6
43 http://www.slate.com/articles/life/food/2008/09/whats_in_a_number.html
44 https://www.fiscal.treasury.gov/fsreports/rpt/finrep/fr/fr_index.htm
45 http://www.politifact.com/truth-o-meter/statements/2016/jan/13/barack-obama/obama-us-spends-more-military-next-8-nations-combi/
46 https://obamawhitehouse.archives.gov/the-press-office/2014/06/20/fact-sheet-economic-challenge-posed-declining-pollinator-populations
47 http://www.goodfruit.com
48 http://developingchild.harvard.edu/science/key-concepts/toxic-stress/
49 http://www.rwjf.org/content/dam/farm/reports/surveys_and_polls/2014/rwjf414295
50 http://www.hamiltonproject.org/papers/money_lightens_the_load
51 http://www.cnn.com/2015/07/22/health/meditate-at-work/index.html
52 https://www.mindful.org/why-mindfulness-belongs-in-the-classroom/
53 http://momentousinstitute.org/services/momentous-school
54 https://www.nps.gov/stli/learn/historyculture/abolition.htm
55 Dictionary.com
56 USmoney.US
57 https://www.nps.gov/stli/learn/historyculture/abolition.htm
58 http://www.slavevoyages.org

59 http://www.civil-war.net/census.asp?census=Total
60 https://www.aaas.org/page/historical-trends-federal-rd
61 Wikipedia
62 https://www.cnbc.com/2016/05/17/its-a-disgrace-this-is-how-much-more-ceos-make-than-workers.html
63 http://fortune.com/2016/07/15/ceo-pay-2/
64 https://www.forbes.com/sites/laurengensler/2016/06/16/one-percent-by-state-income-inequality/
65 https://www.theatlantic.com/business/archive/2016/03/brookings-1-percent/473478/
66 https://www.nasa.gov/content/finding-life-beyond-earth-is-within-reach
67 https://www.usmint.gov/wordpress/wp-content/uploads/2017/02/2016AnnualReport.pdf
68 Quoted from The Collected works of Abraham Lincoln, edited by R. Basler (1953) by Stephen Zarlenga in The Lost Science of Money, (2002, p. 458)
69 A Resource of War by E.G. Spaulding (1971, p. 108) cited by Stephen Zarlenga in The Lost Science of Money (2002, p. 456).
70 https://www.dhs.gov/blue-campaign/what-human-trafficking
71 https://www.theatlantic.com/politics/archive/2016/02/how-sex-trafficking-goes-unnoticed-in-america/470166/
72 http://www.ilo.org/global/about-the-ilo/newsroom/news/WCMS_243201/lang--en/index.htm
73 https://www.bls.gov/opub/btn/volume-4/movies-music-sports-entertainment-spending.htm
74 http://www.marketwatch.com/story/the-nfl-made-13-billion-last-season-see-how-it-stacks-up-against-other-leagues-2016-07-01
75 https://www.sbnation.com/nfl/2015/7/20/9006401/nfl-teams-revenue-tv-deal-7-billion
76 http://gazettereview.com/2017/03/average-nfl-player-salary/
77 http://www.nydailynews.com/sports/football/cowboys-nfl-valuable-team-4-2-billion-article-1.2793374
78 https://thinkprogress.org/7-things-we-could-have-spent-12-billion-on-instead-of-new-sports-stadiums-96da6929049f/
79 http://commonsenseeconomics.com/wp-content/uploads/Sacrificing_Lives_for_Profits_CSE-1.pdf
80 https://fred.stlouisfed.org/series/PSAVERT
81 https://hbr.org/2014/09/profits-without-prosperity
82 The Divine Right of Capital: Dethroning the Corporate aristocracy by Marjorie Kelly (2001)
83 http://www.nationalgeographic.com/environment/global-warming/deforestation/
84 https://www.worldwildlife.org/threats/deforestation
85 https://founders.archives.gov/documents/Franklin/01-01-02-0041
86 http://www.motherjones.com/politics/2011/05/speedup-americans-working-harder-charts/
87 https://www.bls.gov/opub/reports/minimum-wage/2016/home.htm
88 https://www.bls.gov/ncs/ocs/
89 https://www.bls.gov/news.release/archives/union2_01212011.htm

90 https://stats.oecd.org/Index.aspx?DataSet-Code=MIN2AVE -as sorted by Wikipedia, https://en.wikipedia.org/wiki/Minimum_wage

91 https://www.bls.gov/news.release/union2.nr0.htm

92 http://www.history.com/topics/labor

93 https://spinoff.nasa.gov/Spinoff2008/tech_benefits.html

94 http://blogs.findlaw.com/law_and_life/2014/10/who-legally-owns-your-facebook-posts.html

95 https://www.theguardian.com/technology/2017/mar/28/internet-service-providers-sell-browsing-history-house-vote

96 https://www.congress.gov/bill/115TH-congress/senate-joint-resolution/34/all-actions?overview=closed&q=%7B%22roll-call-vote%22%3A%22all%22%7D

97 http://www.frbsf.org/education/publications/doctor-econ/2009/december/subprime-mortgage-statistics/

98 http://www.npr.org/templates/story/story.php?storyId=12561184

99 https://en.wikipedia.org/wiki/Asch_conformity_experiments

100 https://www.ptsd.va.gov/public/ptsd-overview/basics/how-common-is-ptsd.asp

101 https://www.ptsd.va.gov/professional/co-occurring/ptsd-suicide.asp

102 http://articles.latimes.com/2013/dec/20/science/la-sci-sn-veteran-suicide-statistics-20131219

103 https://www.secretservice.gov/about/history/events/

104 https://en.wikipedia.org/wiki/White-collar_crime

105 http://time.com/money/4829684/shoplifting-fraud-retail-survey/

106 https://www.theatlantic.com/magazine/archive/2016/05/why-luck-matters-more-than-you-might-think/476394/

107 https://www.philadelphiafed.org/education/teachers/publications/symbols-on-american-money/

108 Blockchain Revolution; How the technology behind bitcoin is changing money, business, and the world by Don and Alex Tapscott (2016).

109 US Money by Virginia Hammon (2018)

110 http://www.drugscience.org/Archive/bcr2/MJcropReport_2006.pdf

111 https://www.entrepreneur.com/article/290669#

112 https://www.quilts.com/assets/qia_summary.pdf

Image Credits:
Background fabric texture by Subtle Patterns.
https://www.toptal.com/designers/subtlepatterns/
Modified icons from https://www flaticon.com